Becoming Sugar Plum

By Elizabeth Odell Catlett and Heather Stahl Katz

Illustrated by Ellen Cunningham

Text ©2015 By Elizabeth Odell Catlett & Heather Katz
Illustrations ©2015 By Ellen Cunningham

All rights reserved.

No part of this book may be reproduced, stored in a retrievable system, or transmitted by any means without the written permission of the authors. This is a work of fiction. All of the characters, names, incidents, organizations, and dialogue in this novel are either the product of the authors' imagination or are used fictitiously.

Published by CreateSpace, an Amazon Company, 11/20/15

ISBN: 978-1519265968

First Edition, 2015

www.becomingsugarplum.com

Wishing you Sugar Plum dreams...

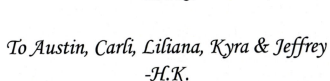

To Estelle & Ryan
-E.O.C.

To Austin, Carli, Liliana, Kyra & Jeffrey
-H.K.

And to our parents,
Ellen & Alan,
Lynn & Sam

With Speacial Thanks to:

Ellen Cunningham
Ryan Catlett
Paula Ross
Lynn Joslin
&
The Board of Directors at Metropolitan Ballet Theatre

Introduction

The classical ballet, *The Nutcracker*, was first performed at the Mariinsky Theatre in St. Petersburg, Russia on December 18, 1892.

Choreographer, Marius Petipa, commissioned Pyotr Illyich Tchaikovsky, a famous Russian composer, to create an original score based on Alexandre Dumas' adaptation of E.T.A. Hoffmann's story of *The Nutcracker and the Mouse King*.

In 2013, Elizabeth Odell Catlett, co-authored a prequel to *The Nutcracker* with a fellow dancer, Heather Stahl Katz, in hopes that their story would be set to an original, musical composition and staged as a classical ballet.

In March of 2016, the Metropolitan Ballet Theatre of Gaithersburg, Maryland—under the artistic direction of Elizabeth Odell Catlett, is scheduled to premiere *Becoming Sugar Plum*. This ballet in two acts is based on the adaptation of the book-*Becoming Sugar Plum*, with an original score composed by Alexandra Bryant.

Preface

LONG ago, there lived a peaceful and unified kingdom of flying fairies, mystical goblins, dancing sweets and other curious creatures. Arguments between the fairies and the goblins led to an era of war until finally, an agreement was made to divide the entire kingdom into three separate lands: Fairyland, the Land of Goblins, and the Land of Sweets. Crossing the fixed border between Fairyland and the Land of Goblins was strictly forbidden.

There once lived a beautiful fairy, Queen Violet, who ruled a land of magical fairies and curious creatures. The fairy queen cared for her land and all of its creatures, but dreamed of much more. So each dark night, the bold Queen Violet crossed into the forbidden Land of Goblins to see her secret love— King Dross.

As Queen Violet and King Dross' love grew, so, too, did their fear of being discovered by their opposing lands.

One fateful evening, Queen Violet flew beyond the strict border, and into the Land of Goblins. In the eerie forest, her beloved King Dross secretly awaited her arrival. He reached out to embrace her and tears flooded her eyes.

"Oh, my dearest King, how can I ever live without you?"

Leaning away, he asked, "My Queen—why? What is wrong?"

She sobbed, "I'm afraid the dreaded time has come. I must leave you, never to return. If anyone sees us together, the peace between our lands will be lost!"

Although King Dross was unhappy, he knew Queen Violet was right. He pulled her in close, and they danced one final time.

"I have a gift for you," said Queen Violet to King Dross.

With her delicate fingers, she gripped a small chain from around her neck and gently lifted the necklace over her head. A brilliant pendant now rested in her open palms. The fairy queen trembled as she broke the pendant in half. She presented one part to King Dross and held fast to the other.

"Please accept this as a token of my eternal love," said the queen.

King Dross nodded sadly. Then before the sun rose, he kissed her farewell.

The King watched the Queen of Fairyland fly off into the distance.

"If only I had wings to follow you, Queen Violet," he cried.

Like the pendant, King Dross' heart was split in two. His misery turned to endless rage.

In time, his land once full of happy goblins, transformed into a land full of bitter creatures. The Land of Goblins, now evil, would come to be known as the Bitter Land.

Many years later, in the nearby Land of Sweets, there lived a handsome prince. He ruled from his splendid castle filled with dancing Meringues, Lollies, Gumdrops and Petit Fours. Every day, the dancing sweets entertained the prince in the castle's grand ballroom.

One afternoon, while the sweets danced for the prince, uninvited guests seeped beneath the castle doors. The shadowy creatures went unnoticed. One by one, the mysterious thieves snatched the dancing Meringues, Lollies, Gumdrops, and Petit Fours. By day's end, the prince called upon his loyal messenger, Cotton Candy.

"Cotton Candy, where have all my sweets gone? The Land of Sweets may be in terrible danger!"

"Prince, I am wondering the same thing. They are nowhere to be found!"

The poor prince pled silently for answers to his troubles. Exhausted, he collapsed into a deep slumber.

Reverie, the mystical dream fairy, heard the prince's call for help. She flew the long distance from Fairyland and entered his dream.

"Prince, perhaps I can be of some assistance. There is another fairy I wish for you to meet."

"I am listening, Dream Fairy," said the prince in his sleep. "I fear for my land and the safety of my precious sweets. More and more Meringues, Lollies, Gumdrops and Petit Fours are disappearing each day. I fear something or someone is stealing them. My castle and grounds are crumbling. Please help."

"Look," said Reverie, and a vision began to appear. An enchanting plum-colored fairy without wings stepped out from a foggy pink mist.

The plum-colored fairy danced with the prince and his fluffy Meringues, luscious Lollies, gooey Gumdrops and delectable Petit Fours. The prince caught but a glimpse, for the breathtaking creature without wings quickly whirled out of his reach and out of his dream.

"You must find this rare plum-colored fairy, Prince," said Reverie. "She holds the key to finding your missing sweets and more."

Then, Reverie fluttered away.

The prince awoke startled and wondered, *"Who was that beautiful, plum-colored fairy?"*

He summoned his messenger, the loyal Cotton Candy.

"Cotton Candy," he said, as he pointed out the castle window, "soar to Fairyland and find me the beautiful plum-colored fairy, born with no wings. Beg her to come to the Land of Sweets at once!"

So, Cotton Candy quickly flew off to find her.

Soon, Cotton Candy arrived in Fairyland. Reverie, the dream fairy, was the first fairy to greet her.

"The prince has sent me to Fairyland to search for the rarest of fairies—the one born with no wings. Can you help me find her?"

With a hint of a smile, Reverie replied, "I've been expecting you! Come with me, and we shall find the fairy you seek."

Together, they began their trek through the glistening fields filled with fairies that joyfully danced for their new visitor.

First, they met Viridescent, the green blossom fairy, along with all her dancing, jeweled-blue periwinkles. Before too long, they also met Aria, a petite yellow-song fairy, who arrived with her flock of hummingbirds.

"Helloooooooo, it's nice to meet you," sang Aria.

"What brings you to Fairyland?" she sang again.

"The prince's sweets are disappearing from his land. He has sent me to find the plum-colored fairy with no wings," said Cotton Candy.

"Princess Plum?" asked Aria.

"Princess? She's a real princess?" asked the surprised Cotton Candy.

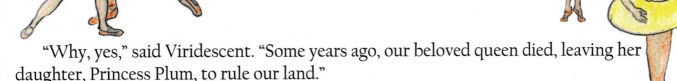

"Why, yes," said Viridescent. "Some years ago, our beloved queen died, leaving her daughter, Princess Plum, to rule our land."

Aria chimed, "I can lead you to our sandy shores. Maybe the princess is there."

Cotton Candy gladly agreed.

Once at the seashore, Maryn, the blue-water fairy, and her school of dolphins, swam to meet them.

"Hello, my friends. What brings you here?" Maryn asked. "Do you need a short getaway by the sea?"

"That would be lovely," sang Aria, "but we are looking for Princess Plum."

"You've just missed her," said Maryn.

Ember, the red-fire fairy, heard the commotion and flew over to greet the new visitor.

"I know how to find her," said Ember. "Just follow the lights. The princess left with my teensy, weensy fireflies."

    As night fell, Ember led Cotton Candy and all her new friends back to the periwinkle fields. There, in the distance, twinkling lights flickered all about.
    The glowing cloud fascinated Cotton Candy. She moved in to get a closer look. Within the midst of the shining fireflies, was the beautiful and sparkling plum-colored fairy.

"Greetings, Princess Plum. I am Cotton Candy, the messenger, from the Land of Sweets. It's an honor to meet you."

Cotton Candy told the tale of the prince's woes and then pleaded for Princess Plum to travel to the castle to help the prince.

Reverie then appeared and said, "Princess Plum, you must accept the prince's request, for it has been foretold that only you can save his land of disappearing sweets."

"I can't leave Fairyland. Who will look after our land?" questioned Princess Plum.

Reverie interrupted, "I will watch over Fairyland. I promised your mother, Queen Violet, to always take care of you and our land."

"How will I get to the Land of Sweets? I don't have any wings to fly," the princess sighed.

"You and your fairies will go to the prince on foot. You can take the secret passage through Bitter Land at night, hide in the forest, and then cross into the Land of Sweets at dawn."

The princess gasped, "Crossing into Bitter Land will break the longstanding peace agreement. Fairies are forbidden there."

Reverie replied, "Trust me."

Princess Plum understood the great risks, but somehow she knew that she had to help the prince and his suffering sweets.

Accepting Cotton Candy's request, the princess and her fairies prepared for their daring journey through the Bitter Land.

Cotton Candy returned to the castle in the Land of Sweets.

"Prince," said Cotton Candy, "the rare fairy born with no wings is a true princess, Princess Plum. She will come to you, but first she and her fairies must walk through the Bitter Land."

Surprised, the prince said, "Cotton Candy, it is said that when the Goblin King Dross lost his beloved a long time ago, he and his entire land turned bitter. I must help Princess Plum cross the forbidden land that rests between us. The Bitter Land is too dangerous for a fairy that cannot fly."

And so, the prince set out to find Princess Plum and help her safely reach his Land of Sweets.

    As the fairies carefully traveled through the Goblin forest, they heard the sound of footsteps and saw movement in the bushes.

    "Did you hear that?" whispered a frightened Aria.

    "Yes. What was it?" asked Viridescent.

    Ember spotted the scraggly shrubs around them. "I heard the rustling over there. It looks as though the forest has restless legs and reaching arms."

    "Princess Plum, let's hurry out of here! These bushes are alive," trembled Maryn.

    "Shhh...my fairies," said the brave princess. "Who's out there? Speak up. We mean you no harm."

    An area of thistle branches opened up, and a young man, both tall and handsome appeared. The fairies leaped to hide behind the thistle berry bushes.

    "Who are you?" demanded Princess Plum.

"I am the Prin—," he said. But before he could finish, beastly shadows lunged from the bushes, seized the prince and swiftly hauled him away.

The poison thistle berry bushes stirred in response. They stretched out their branches and plucked up each fairy to trap them in their knotted limbs. The bushes and their new fairy prisoners slowly followed the shadows and the prince as they made their way through the forest to the Goblin King's lair.

Inside the lair, the evil King Dross watched his creeping shadows dance around the tied up prince, but he soon grew bored. He cast the prince aside and called upon his new collection of prisoner sweets to take the dance floor instead.

The prince couldn't believe his eyes!

"YOU stole my sweets?" the prince asked the hideous Goblin King.

"Your sweets are now mine. They shall dance for me and for my bitter creatures whenever I choose," said the angry king as he signaled the sweets to start their waltz.

Then the lair doors flew open, startling the sweets and abruptly ending their dance. The bushes dragged and tugged the captured fairies through the hall and across the king's lair.

"What are they doing here?" King Dross shouted at first sight of the intruders.

Princess Plum pushed her way through the thistle berry bushes and gracefully stepped forward.

"Bring me that fairy—the one with no wings," said King Dross.
The Goblin King studied Princess Plum. He almost smiled at the sight of her—something he hadn't done in a long time. She seemed familiar. The king was flooded with memories of love, happiness, and then heartache. The more he looked at the plum-colored fairy, the more she reminded him of his once beloved Queen Violet.

The evil Goblin King then screeched. "Shadows, tie up the new prisoners who have trespassed into our land!" He turned back with rage, "Plum Fairy, I command you to dance for me until your last breath!"

The fairies cried with fear, the shadows cheered and the prince gasped. The prince wanted to rescue the plum-colored fairy, but he couldn't break free from his ropes.

Who could save Princess Plum?

Princess Plum demanded, "I will only dance for you in exchange for the freedom of my fairies and the prince. You must also agree to return the stolen sweets."

Spellbound by her courage, King Dross said, "Fine. Agreed. I will free them, but you are not to leave. You are mine. Dance!"

The prisoners were released, but stayed and watched in fear as the dance began. Princess Plum leapt as though she could fly, and turned on her toes as though her feet never touched the floor. Her glorious movements amazed King Dross and the prince.

As the music sped up, the princess began to turn and turn and turn as if under a spell.

And then she turned some more until, "CLINK!" An object fell to the floor. The music stopped and Princess Plum collapsed. Lying on the ground before her was something shiny.

King Dross bent over and picked up a broken pendant.

"What is this?" he asked.

The plum-colored fairy said with tears in her eyes, "My mother gave it to me when I was a little fairy girl as a token of her love. Please give it back to me. It is all I have to remember her by."

"Who are you?" he demanded.

"I am Princess Plum of Fairyland," she said.

    The teary Goblin King pulled out a broken pendant from inside his robe. He placed the halves together, and like interlocking pieces to a puzzle, they made a perfect fit.
    "Could it be? Are you my daughter?" King Dross asked.
    Princess Plum realized that the missing half of her pendant belonged to her father, the Goblin King.
    "Now, I finally understand why I was born without wings," she said.
    King Dross was joyous once again, for his beloved Fairy Queen Violet had given him a most magical and beautiful daughter.

The prince was overwhelmed with joy that the Goblin King was going to return his Meringues, Lollies, Gumdrops and Petit Fours safely to the Land of Sweets.

The prince wanted to formally introduce himself to the princess.

"Princess Plum, I am the Prince of the Land of Sweets. Thank you for your bravery. You have saved my sweets!"

King Dross approached the prince.

"Prince, please forgive me for causing such pain to you and your sweets. Now, after discovering my daughter, I only wish for peace among the three lands as they once were before the wars."

"King Dross," said the prince, "I agree with you. It is time that our people live happily together."

King Dross nodded and said, "I am old and my daughter, Princess Plum, will one day become ruler of the Land of Goblins and Fairyland. Let us unite all of our lands under one kingdom as they once were in olden days."

The prince shook the king's hand.

  King Dross and the prince admired Princess Plum, for her strength, bravery, and kindness had healed all the lands.
  Together they said, "Princess Plum, you have saved the Land of Sweets and have returned joy to the Land of Goblins. Reverie's vision has come true. We will never be able to thank you enough for all the good you have done. Accept this gift as a symbol of our appreciation."
  Princess Plum opened the box, and inside, she found a sparkling, jeweled crown.
  "How beautiful!" exclaimed Princess Plum.

"We would like to unite our three lands under one kingdom as they once were long, long ago. It would be an honor if you would rule over the newly-unified Kingdom of Sweets," said the prince and King Dross.

"The Kingdom of Sweets?" asked the princess with a smile. "It would be my honor and a privilege."

"We shall call you Princess Plum, the Sugar Plum Fairy," said King Dross.

The inhabitants of all the lands harmoniously gathered in the Kingdom of Sweets to celebrate their new ruler. King Dross, the fairies, the dancing sweets, and all of kingdom's curious creatures watched as the prince officially crowned the Sugar Plum Fairy, ruler over all the lands!

And, at long last, there was peace and happiness everywhere.

Made in the USA
Middletown, DE
11 February 2016